DEALING
with
DEPRESSION

Hope & Healing for a Brighter Future

by Drs. Steve & Rebecca Wilke

This information is not meant to replace the professional and personal relationship between doctor and patient that is often necessary to assess, diagnose, and treat physical and/or mental disorders. Please do not substitute this material for such a relationship. We encourage you to seek the wise counsel of a qualified professional for a thorough and complete examination of the issues facing you. Referral sources have been included in the back of this book, or you can contact us directly at Sonkist Ministries for further assistance.

Dealing with Depression: Hope and Healing for a Brighter Future

Leadon Publishing
P.O. Box 503377
San Diego, CA 92150
www.leadon.biz

Cover Design by Gary Christenson
Interior Design by Pine Hill Graphics
Editor Hannah Selleck

Publisher's Cataloging-in-Publication Data
(Provided by Cassidy Cataloguing Services, Inc.)

Wilke, Steve (Stephen D.)

Dealing with depression / Steve and Rebecca Wilke. -- San Diego, CA : Leadon Pub., c2010.

p. ; cm.

ISBN: 13-digit: 978-0-9673989-1-4 ; 10-digit: 0-9673989-1-6
First published by Sonkist Ministries, c2000.
Includes bibliographical references.

1. Depression, Mental. 2. Depression, Mental--Religious aspects. 3. Depression, Mental--Treatment. I. Wilke, Rebecca Lynn. II. Title.

RC537 .W54 2010
616.85/27--dc22 1009

Library of Congress Card Number: 99-68053

Printed in the United States of America.

Why are you downcast, O my soul?
Why so disturbed within me?
Put your hope in God,
for I will yet praise him,
my Savior and my God.

Psalm 42:5–6a

Table of Contents

Dealing with Depression: Hope & Healing for a Brighter Future

Tina and Scott came to our counseling clinic in search of help. Now in their late forties, the couple wanted to keep their marriage together, but they were desperately trying to recover from Tina's affair with a co-worker. They'd both had previous marriages, and Tina overcame depression in her past. The fallout of the affair had sent her reeling into despair again, and Scott was sinking quickly, too. After several weeks of counseling, the unthinkable happened. Scott died of a heart attack. Tina was devastated by her loss, and the guilt of her actions only intensified her depression.

Keith epitomized the successful, self-made man. Yet his multi-millions, designer suit, and Rolex couldn't make up for the losses he'd dealt with during his developmental years. Neglect, molestation, and physical abuse had characterized Keith's childhood experiences, and in addition to his traumatized past, numerous physical problems complicated his current symptoms. Because of his professional successes, outwardly he appeared to have it all, but none of his friends or colleagues knew the inner turmoil Keith battled every day. His third marriage was failing, and his only son struggled with his parents' separation. Keith felt that his world was falling apart and could never be rebuilt. He was extremely depressed and thought that it might be better to die so that he wouldn't have to struggle any longer.

Mark told himself that he had a pretty great life, so he didn't understand why he felt so down all the time. After all, he was his own boss, made his own schedule, and answered to no one, and despite the usual ups and downs of the economy, business had been going well. His kids were grown, so he finally had plenty of free time to do the things he wanted. In fact, he'd just purchased his first boat, and he and his wife were traveling more together, but Mark had to admit that none of this fun seemed to make him happy. He felt depressed most days for no apparent reason; his wife had commented on the change in his personality. She was planning a big birthday bash for his fifty-sixth birthday to cheer him up, but he wasn't even looking forward to seeing his friends at the party. All Mark wanted to do was get the spark back in his life that he once had.

Lori wasn't sleeping well, and she felt anxious much of the time she was awake. She'd been dealing with too many stresses lately—so many that she had to quit her job. Her father had died a few months prior, and now her mother was struggling with health issues. Her

Depression impacts people in all walks of life.

eldest daughter had just gone away to college, leaving her alone with a husband she didn't enjoy being around. So she started drinking again. Lori knew that she shouldn't drink at all; she'd been raised in an alcoholic family and had already had problems herself, but she was lonely at home, worn out from taking care of her mother, and scared about facing her own illness and death one day.

Depression truly is a deceptive enemy. It sneaks in subtly and attacks its unsuspecting victims. This enemy is not selective; it impacts people in all walks of life. Depression robs men and women of their joy, breaking their spirit with its ever-tightening grip. Sometimes this enemy attacks quickly; other times it lingers for years. Extreme circumstances can cause hallucinations, delusions, and thoughts of suicide. On occasion, depression is obvious; yet at other times, it advances unnoticed, striking in the most unexpected ways and leaving its victims suffering from debilitating symptoms. The stranglehold that depression can place on people can seem unbreakable!

Dealing with Depression is a tool designed to help you fight this enemy and to aid you in finding hope and healing in the days ahead.

One of the first things you need to know is that you are not alone in this battle! Many men and women have dealt with depression. Here are just a few: Martin Luther, John Bunyan, Charles Spurgeon, J. B. Phillips, Søren Kierkegaard, Ernest Hemingway,

Depression is no respecter of persons. It has been called the common cold of emotional disorders and it appears to be on the rise.

Winston Churchill, and Abraham Lincoln. More recently, journalist Mike Wallace, former First Lady Barbara Bush, and retired astronaut Buzz Aldrin have acknowledged their experiences with depression.

Psychologist Siang-Yang Tan once said, "Depression is no respecter of persons. It has been called the common cold of emotional disorders and it appears to be on the rise." Studies on human

One in five of us will suffer from depression at some point in our lives.

behavior reveal that **one in five** of us will suffer from depression at some point in our lives (*Christian Counseling Today*, 1995). About **18.8 million Americans experience some form of depressive disorder** (Substance Abuse and Mental Health Services Administration). In fact, major depressive disorders affect approximately **14.8 million American adults**. This represents about **6.7%**

of the U.S. population ages 18 and older in a given year. **Major depressive disorder is the leading cause of disability in the U.S. for ages 15-44** (National Institute of Mental Health).

Since many of us will be impacted by depression—either by experiencing it ourselves or through someone we care about—it's critical that we learn how to effectively cope with this disorder. The good news is that there is help for battling depression, and there is hope for a much brighter future. ***Dealing with Depression*** will provide you with the information you need to make sound decisions on what course to take in the healing process. More importantly, God has a purpose for your life and will give you the strength you need to fight and find the road to recovery.

What Is Depression?

All of us at some time or other have experienced a mild form of depression—the condition of feeling down or despondent. **Mild depression** is a common human experience, but clinical depression's impact is much more debilitating, so it is important to

> ***All of us at some time or other have experienced a mild form of depression.***

differentiate between the two. **Clinical depression** occurs when sadness turns to such unhappiness that you can't fulfill daily roles and responsibilities. A lack of vitality, a lingering sense of dejection, and the loss of interest in many of life's activities characterize this deeper level of clinical depression.

> ***You can no more reason yourself into cheerfulness than you can reason yourself an extra six inches in height. You can only be better prepared.***

Depression can be experienced in numerous ways. It can be temporary and mild, or completely overwhelming. Though millions struggle with depression each year, it is still misunderstood and often ignored or left untreated. Sadly, everyone involved suffers because depression impacts family, friends, co-workers, and other people in an individual's sphere of influence. But there is hope for recovery! There are specific steps that you can take to alleviate and overcome these intense feelings of sadness and despondency.

Though millions struggle with depression each year, it is still misunderstood and often ignored or left untreated.

What Causes Depression?

Oswald Chambers (2008) once said that "if we were never depressed we would not be alive—only material things don't suffer depression. If human beings were not capable of depression, we would have no capacity for happiness and exaltation."

Feeling down is as natural as life itself because it's a normal response to stress. However, with clinical depression, these feelings become severe and long-lasting. So, what actually causes depression?

> ***If we were never depressed we would not be alive—only material things don't suffer depression.***

The answer is fairly complex. Sometimes an event triggers depression, while other times nothing in particular occurs. Depression is unique to each individual who experiences it, so it's not always easy to give general explanations; however, there are some key contributing factors. These include:

Biological or Genetic
Environmental or Situational
Interpersonal
Physiological or Biochemical
Psychological or Emotional
Spiritual

Let's take a look at these categories to get a better understanding of each one.

Biological/Genetic

Researchers now realize that imbalances in brain chemistry can cause depression. Sensitive chemicals in your brain, called *neurotransmitters*, can become disturbed, and when they do, depression may occur. Scientists know that people suffering from depressive

Researchers now realize that imbalances in brain chemistry can cause depression.

illnesses seem to have too many or too few neurotransmitters of a certain type. Problems with brain chemistry may be the result of inherited characteristics. If members in your family have experienced depression, then you might also be genetically predisposed; thus, depression becomes a physical problem based upon genetics. However, while depression can be passed down through the generations, it can also occur in families with no history of depression.

Environmental/Situational

A stressful environment can create the potential for depression. Today's ever-changing culture can certainly impact our emotional capacities. Deteriorating families, divorce, unresolved conflict, violence, chemical dependency, the secularization of society, racial tension, and poverty all contribute heavily to emotional problems. The

Most of the problems we see in our clinic have their origins in personal relationships that have gone awry.

use of alcohol or drugs (prescription or illegal) can increase despondency. People also enter our clinic completely overwhelmed by a lack of support from their families and communities. In addition, major life changes often cause depression. The bottom line is that the world we live in greatly impacts the way we feel about ourselves.

Interpersonal

Most of the problems we see in our clinic have their origins in personal relationships that have gone awry. Interpersonal relationships—or the lack of them—account for a major portion of depression cases. Family problems, a lack of connectedness within communities, loneliness, marital conflict, and work relationships all impact the way we think and feel on a daily basis.

Physiological/Biochemical

The physiological or biochemical component of depression cannot be overlooked. We have already discussed how brain chemistry affects the way we feel from day to day. Any dramatic fluctuation in our neurotransmitters impacts our mood and life experiences. A number of medical conditions can also contribute to our psychological functioning. Strokes, thyroid problems, and lack of physical exercise are just a few factors that can impact our well-being. Medications such as birth control pills, high blood pressure medication, and steroids can create psychological and emotional problems. Plus, many of the people we treat don't take good care of themselves. Lack of sleep, a poor diet, nutritional deficiencies, exhaustion, over-work, traumatic injuries, and medical illnesses strain emotional well-being.

Psychological/Emotional

Simply put, some people are prone to depression. We've discussed how our biological histories can contribute to depression.

Certain medical conditions, drugs with negative side effects, or imbalanced brain chemistry can also contribute to this situation.

Yet there are some individuals whose psychological makeup leaves them vulnerable to depression. They often have low self-esteem, lack self-confidence, and they view their world negatively.

Some people are prone to depression.

They consider the world a bad place, and they think that people treat them poorly. Isolation and withdrawal often are a result of these types of feelings.

Terrible family experiences or traumatic events during developmental years can leave us emotionally vulnerable, allowing depression to creep in.

Isolation resulting in loneliness and lack of interpersonal relationships can push some people into a severe depressive cycle. Dr.

Depressive emotions can result from anger turned inward.

Tim LaHaye, in his best-selling book, *How to Win Over Depression* (1996), explains that depressive emotions can result from anger turned inward. Many people try to cope with intense emotions by internalizing their feelings. They bury experiences deep inside instead of dealing with those feelings directly. Internalizing emotions is a huge threat to overall well-being.

Spiritual

We are often asked if spiritual issues can be connected to depression; the answer is yes! We believe that all of life's dilemmas can and should be considered from a spiritual perspective. Many problems in modern-day society stem directly from attempts to secularize our lives and deny the spiritual nature of our humanity.

We live in a world that is far from perfect, so depression happens, though it certainly isn't what God had in mind for His creation! Sometimes depression can stem directly from ongoing sin in our lives. Anger, bitterness, resentment, hostility, and

We believe that all of life's dilemmas can and should be considered from a spiritual perspective.

other intense emotions, if left unchecked, can develop into full-blown depression. The Bible is also full of examples of trials, tribulations, and spiritual warfare. The resulting stress and pain from these experiences often lead to depression. Throughout the Psalms, we discover David constantly wrestling with the emotional and spiritual aspects of life (Spurgeon, 2004).

People are spiritual beings, and the world we live in is full of challenges and difficulties. While there are numerous causes of depression, part of the healing process must involve caring for the spiritual aspect of a person's life. In his book, *Depression: A Stubborn Darkness—Light for the Path,* Welch (2004) contends that faith must be interlaced with therapies in order for depression to be properly addressed. (We will discuss more of the spiritual aspects of depression later in the book).

Look back over this inventory of factors that contribute to depression, and see if you fall into any of these categories. Knowing the causes of depression can help you bring balance back into your life and increase your effectiveness in dealing with this problem.

Faith must be interlaced with therapies in order for depression to be properly addressed.

Who Gets Depressed?

People of all ages and in all walks of life suffer from depression. All races and ethnic groups are impacted. (And yes, even Christians get depressed!) Many men and women assume that only non-believers or those who have fallen away from God will deal with depression. This is a myth and a false assumption that creates all kinds of pain in the lives of innocent people of faith. Emotional suffering is not always an indication of shallow spirituality.

Emotional suffering is not always an indication of shallow spirituality.

Believe it or not, even **babies and children** can be depressed. For instance, medical professionals describe "failure to thrive" babies as those who struggle to survive for a variety of reasons, including physical and emotional neglect (Krugman & Dubowitz, 2003; KidsHealth.org). This situation can be extremely serious, and problems from this type of condition can carry on into and through adulthood.

Babies and children can be depressed.

According to researchers, the increase in antidepressant use among children continues to rise (Delate, Gelenberg, Simmons & Motheral, 2004). Behavioral and academic problems at school, as well as difficult peer relationships are signs that may indicate the presence of childhood depression, with unresolved and ongoing family conflict often cited as a major contributing factor.

Adolescents can also become deeply depressed. Often teenagers cry for help by acting out in two ways: the first method is to gain attention by dramatic behavior, including rebelliousness, rule-breaking, inappropriate school conduct, a drop in academic performance, academic underachievement, alcohol or drug use, and promiscuous behavior. Second, some teenagers withdraw completely when they are struggling emotionally. Irritability, isolation, change in relational habits, loss of interest in activities, and abrupt changes in mood are common signs of teenage depression. Adolescents also go through tremendous physical and psychological changes, which can affect their moods. Social pressures at

Teen suicide is the third leading cause of death for this age group.

their stage of life, as well as hormonal shifts contribute to changes that can be completely overwhelming for teens. Most seriously, teen suicide is the third leading cause of death for this age group. In 2001, this resulted in 30, 622 deaths (FamilyFirstAid.org). Adults must look for signs of depression and seek help for teenagers who exhibit symptoms as soon as possible.

Depression might strike **young adults** as they struggle to successfully balance their new roles and responsibilities. The social pressures to make friends or date and marry can be overwhelming. Occupational concerns about a career or the new pressures of starting a family and parenting can be extremely stressful. Added to these concerns is the underlying need to prove that they can make it on their own.

Middle-aged adults often suffer from depression, usually in relation to several specific problems. Mid-life crises become more than a cliché when people begin to wonder if they have met their life goals. Men and women also face the "empty nest syndrome" as children grow up and leave home to attend college or begin life on their own. Menopause, physical problems, and psychological changes impact adults as they mature. All of these situations

30% of women are diagnosed with depression, while men account for about 15% of identified cases.

can lead to depression, especially when compounded by physiological factors. It is interesting to note that approximately 30% of women are diagnosed with depression, while men account for about 15% of identified cases (National Institute of Mental Health). Many men and women are often too embarrassed to seek help (National Mental Health Association).

Deep sadness, loneliness, death of a spouse or friends, and feelings of isolation dramatically affect many **elderly adults**. This age group has experienced an increase in the incidence of depres-

Depression is estimated to become the second largest killer after heart disease by 2020, and studies now reveal that it is a contributing factor to fatal coronary disease.

sion. People are living longer, but this does not mean their quality of life is better. Many seniors deal with severe medical problems and lack the support they need. Sadly, many think they are a burden to their families, and several are made to feel this way!

15% of depressed people will commit suicide.

Please note: Women are more likely to be diagnosed with depression, but many men also struggle with this disorder. Both genders are susceptible to depression, and both need assistance overcoming their dilemma before the situation becomes more serious. **Depression is estimated to become the second largest killer after heart disease by 2020**, and studies now reveal that it is a contributing factor to fatal coronary disease (World Health Organization). In addition, **15% of depressed people will commit suicide (**Agency for Healthcare Research and Quality).

Anyone can be a candidate for depression.

Anyone can be a candidate for depression. Intelligent, successful, wealthy, talented, educated, and spiritual individuals can suffer its symptoms, so all of us must become more aware of this disorder and know how to deal with depression as effectively as possible.

Signs & Symptoms of Depression

Read this checklist and mark any categories that apply to you or someone you know. This could help determine if depression is the problem that you are currently facing.

- I feel sad and/or irritable much of the time.
- I don't feel pleasure from life like I used to.
- My appetite has changed over the last month.
- I have lost or gained weight, and others have noticed.
- My sleep patterns have changed. I sleep too much, or not enough.
- I am tired all the time.
- I have no energy for everyday activities.
- I feel guilty, helpless, or worthless most of the time.
- I can't concentrate, remember things, or make decisions.
- I am restless or my activity level has decreased.
- I often think about death.
- I have tried to physically hurt myself.

If several of these apply to you, then you may be suffering from symptoms of depression.

Learn to Identify the Early Signs of Depression

Most of us are reluctant to give ourselves a break when under severe stress, and, consequently, our situations worsen. We need to recognize that extra support will be needed during times of duress. Research reveals that there are many events throughout life that can cause serious depression. If any of the following events have occurred in your life—or in the life of someone you care about—then you should seek help to deal with your circumstances. Neglecting to effectively face these major life events can cause serious problems with depression.

- Death of an immediate family member
- Infidelity
- Financial problems
- Loss of job
- Miscarriage
- Infertility
- Separation or divorce
- Unwanted pregnancy
- Unemployment
- Major illness
- Lawsuit
- Family problems
- Death of a friend

Remember, symptoms of depression can vary widely from person to person. Usually depressive symptoms are evident in three distinct categories: ***Feelings***, ***Changes in Behaviors and Attitudes***, and ***Physical Complaints***.

Symptoms of depression can vary widely from person to person. Usually depressive symptoms are evident in three distinct categories: Feelings, Changes in Behaviors and Attitudes, and Physical Complaints.

Depressed Feelings Include:

- Feelings of emptiness
- Feelings of hopelessness
- Loss of pleasurable feelings in activities that typically give pleasure
- Loss of ability to enjoy anything
- Loss of fondness toward family and friends
- Feelings of worthlessness
- Feelings of guilt and shame
- Loss of self-respect
- Loss of self confidence
- Thoughts of suicide
- Thoughts of death

Depressive Behaviors and Attitudes Include:

- Irritability
- Poor concentration
- Poor memory
- Indecisiveness
- Irresponsibility in usual obligations
- Sloppy appearance
- General slowing down
- Crying without knowing why
- Withdrawal

Physical Signs of Depression Include:

- Disturbances in sleeping—early waking, sleep/wake cycle disturbance, sleeping too much or too little

- Loss of energy
- Fatigue
- Loss of appetite
- Weight loss or weight gain
- Unexplained headaches
- Unexplained backaches
- Stomachaches
- Indigestion
- Changes in bowel habits

About 80% of people who experience these depressive symptoms also exhibit symptoms of anxiety.

About 80% of people who experience these depressive symptoms also exhibit symptoms of anxiety, including unrealistic apprehension, fear, and worry. Agitation, irritability, and panic attacks are also often common. In addition, approximately 60% of men and women have physical symptoms that coincide with their anxiety and depression. These include chronic fatigue, chronic pain, and irritable bowel syndrome. Sixty-five percent of these people suffer sleep disturbances, about 20% feel agitated, and 25% have active phobias (unrealistic fears that dramatically impact lifestyle).

60% of men and women have physical symptoms that coincide with their anxiety and depression.

In addition, 17% of men and women report generalized anxiety symptoms and 10% suffer full-blown panic attacks. Anxiety disorders will affect 20% of Americans during the course of their lifetime (United States Department of Health and Human

Services). The combination of depression and anxiety can become debilitating and more difficult to treat successfully, especially as the presence of anxiety often increases the risk of suicide.

Anxiety disorders will affect 20% of Americans during the course of their lifetime.

Please see our book *Answers to Anxiety* for a comprehensive look at how anxiety may impact people, and how help can be found even in the midst of difficult life circumstances.

Are There Different Types of Depression?

How do doctors diagnose the differing forms of depression? Several references can be reviewed to assist in this process. Mental health professionals use the Diagnostic and Statistical Manual (DSM) published by the American Psychiatric Association, which contains all the signs and symptoms of mental health problems. This manual is updated regularly, and currently it can be found as the DSM-IV-TR (2000).

The DSM-IV-TR includes several different types of depression; we will explain seven categories below: ***Normal Depressed Mood, Adjustment Disorder with Depressed Mood, Mild Depression, Major Depression, Bipolar Disorder, Seasonal Affective Disorder and Post-partum Depression***.

Normal Depressed Mood: This reaction is a normal and natural response to the losses in life we all experience. A person may feel sad, lethargic, and, in severe cases, despondent or angry. Loss of sleep, loss of appetite, weight-gain, guilt, or obsessive, repetitive thoughts can develop. Depression is a normal response to dilemmas during certain times of life, but only a reasonable amount of time should be given to a depressive response. At some point, we must be able to move on with our lives. Bad things happen, and life can be tough, but we cannot allow our lives to become permanently paralyzed, or else we cease to live in a meaningful and significant way.

For example, losing a favorite possession can take a day or two to get over, while losing your job might take a few months. The death of a friend or family member might take a year or more. However, if you didn't get a job promotion and find that you can't stop sobbing uncontrollably for days, then you may need help to deal with the situation. If the response to a loss is not balanced—in other words, equal or appropriate to the loss incurred—then asking for and receiving professional assistance is probably in order.

Adjustment Disorder with Depressed Mood: Life is full of adjustments. While many of us face changes rather reluctantly, dealing with transition is essential for successful living. If an experience leaves us feeling down for extended periods of time, we can become increasingly angry and unable to cope with our lives; this is adjustment disorder with depressed mood. This type of depression stems from a life-changing event; for instance: moving to a new city, leaving family behind because of school or a job in another state, or transitioning to a different stage of life. If you or someone you care about is still depressed well after a transition in life, then you might want to consider seeking professional assistance to get through the difficult transitional stage.

Mild Depression (Dysthymia): Dysthymia is an ongoing, low level of depression that can go undetected and untreated for years. The problem is characterized by a long-standing depressed mood, lack of self confidence, and poor self-respect, but it's less intense than a major depression (see below). Mildly depressed people often function adequately, but view themselves as constantly failing in their lives. This type of depression may or may not have a triggering event; frequently there is nothing to blame it on. This can frustrate other people in the depressed person's life, which adds to the dysthymic distress because everyone wants an answer as to what caused the mood change. The qualified care of a professional to help diagnose and treat dysthymia is essential for the recovery process.

A staggering 25% of those who suffer a major depressive episode attempt to kill themselves within five years.

Major Depression: The despair and despondency characterized by this form of depression is life-altering. A person dealing with Major Depression displays a loss of interest in life and is not capable of feeling pleasure in normal, everyday activities. Typically the individual cannot get out of bed, is not able to enjoy sex, and does not eat properly. Other signs, which might not regularly be associated with Major Depression, include weight loss or gain, sleeping too much or not at all, irritability, agitation, chronic indecisiveness, and anxiety.

Any talk of suicide is serious.

One can also suffer this type of serious depression without a triggering event or even feeling "the blues." Besides the terrible misery of depression, there is a serious risk of suicide. A staggering 25% of those who suffer a major depressive episode attempt to kill themselves within five years. Many people think that if someone talks about suicide their chances of hurting themselves are alleviated, but this is far from the case! Men and women who take their lives usually announce their intentions beforehand, yet they aren't taken seriously. ***Any talk of suicide is serious.*** If this situation sounds familiar for you or someone you know, please seek assistance from a mental health professional immediately.

Bipolar Disorder (Manic-Depression): This depressive disorder is characterized by episodes of Major Depression alternating with episodes of high-energy, wildly unrealistic activity, known as Mania. A person might experience many of the symptoms one day, and then be completely without symptoms the next. This individual may be depressed and agitated on one occasion then feel anxious on another. Usually, Bipolar Disorder develops without a clear cause and may not have a triggering event. This disorder is typically inherited, appears later in life, and needs to be treated with medication. These individuals can be a danger to themselves or others and therefore need the immediate attention of a mental health professional.

Signs of Mania may include the following:

- Excessively elevated mood
- Irritability
- Decreased need for sleep
- Increased energy and activity
- Increased talking, walking, and sexual activity
- Rapid and racing thoughts
- Indecisiveness
- Grandiose thoughts
- Easily distracted
- Significant overspending
- Significant irresponsibility

Seasonal Affective Disorder (SAD): Have you ever heard of the "winter blues," the mild or major depression that develops in the fall and clears up in the spring? While a specific cause of SAD remains unknown, reduced sunlight, as well as decreased melatonin (a natural hormone) and serotonin (a brain chemical/neurotransmitter) all seem to be major contributors to this form of depression (MayoClinic.com). In the Northern Hemisphere, the worst months for those with Seasonal Affective Disorder are December, January, and February (or June, July, and August in the Southern Hemisphere). While sometimes subtle in nature, this type of depression can change individuals' normal response to everyday events, but now there are many helpful treatments to overcome Seasonal Affective Disorder.

Postpartum Depression: For some new mothers, the joy of childbirth can be ruined by the presence of post-partum depression. **All moms experience fluctuations in hormones after delivery and can be overwhelmed by the challenges of caring for a new baby.** Their happiness over the arrival of their baby is replaced by short-term sadness. From this large group of women, nearly one in five will become clinically depressed and need professional care. A small percentage of new mothers become so severely depressed that both their health and that of their newborns are in jeopardy. In these extreme cases, hospitalization is often needed for the mothers' and infants' safety. There is a difference between normal postpartum blues and a potentially dangerous post-partum depression, but all forms of depression must be taken seriously, so seek help from professionals trained to diagnose and treat these illnesses.

Additional Concerns: Violence in our communities has become more commonplace over the past several decades. Often the perpetrators are described as depressed human beings who have exhibited significant psychological and emotional problems for years. Please review these warning signs so you can be more aware of potential problems:

Potential Signals of Depression in the Workplace:

- Decreased productivity
- Problems with motivation
- Low morale
- Decreased cooperation
- Decreased safety and increased accidents; carelessness
- Absenteeism
- Complaints of fatigue
- Use and/or abuse of alcohol and drugs

Identifying and understanding the different types of depression can be difficult. Even friends, co-workers, and family members can miss the critical signs of more serious forms of depression. It takes professional assessments to compare and contrast these disorders to arrive at an accurate diagnosis, and the counsel of a qualified mental health professional is needed to determine the appropriate treatment plan so that the road to recovery can begin.

Is There Treatment or a Cure for Depression?

While millions suffer every year from depression, unfortunately about 80% of depressed people are not getting treatment at any one time for a variety of reasons, including symptoms that go undiagnosed (National Healthcare Quality Report, 2003). Sometimes symptoms are blamed on personal weaknesses, or often the individual is so affected that he or she can't reach out for help. When they do seek help, men and women are sometimes misdiagnosed and treated incorrectly. Everyone involved suffers while depression runs rampant.

About 80% of depressed people are not getting treatment at any one time for a variety of reasons, including symptoms that go undiagnosed.

The good news is that all forms of depression can be diagnosed and treated! In fact, the vast majority of people, especially those with severe depression, can feel better within a few weeks of receiving help. About 80% of those with the most severe depression respond rapidly to treatment (National Institute of Mental Health). The first step in successfully dealing with depression is to recognize the warning signs and begin to develop a plan of attack.

There are several different ways that you can start the recovery process. You have already taken a first step in this process by reading our book to educate yourself about depression.

Next, you need to *take action*. If you or someone you know has some of the symptoms of depression, something must be done, and right now! Below are practical suggestions that you can implement immediately.

1) **Seek the assessment and recommendation of a qualified professional.** Nothing can take the place of a thorough, complete consultation with a health care provider. First, get a physical examination from your physician. You want

> ***About 80% of those with the most severe depression respond rapidly to treatment.***

   to rule out any potential medical condition that may be contributing to or causing the depression. Second, get a complete psychiatric assessment from a psychologist, psychiatrist, or mental health professional you can trust. This will give you accurate feedback from a specialist.

2) Begin to **share your feelings** with people close to you. Many people are isolated from the connections and nurturing they need the most. Talk about your depression where you feel safe. Many mental health professionals believe that a supportive social network is essential to physical and emotional healing (Baumeister & Leary, 1995).

3) **Diet and nutrition** are key factors of healing. Depressed people typically don't take very good care of themselves. Your physician can assist you in setting up a healthy nutritional plan as you work through this season of life.

4) **Get some type of cardiovascular exercise**. Mental health experts agree that movement helps enhance the healing process for depressed patients (Blumenthal, et al, 1999). Start by walking 15-20 minutes, and then increase to 30-40 minutes,

four times a week. Run, swim, play racquetball, basketball, jump rope, ride a bike—you get the idea! Please check with your doctor before beginning any exercise program, especially if you've been inactive for some time.

5) **Take time for relationship and recreation.** Depressed individuals find support and encouragement when they're around others and are involved in their favorite activities. Even being out in nature or spending time with pets can elevate your mood (Clay, 2001; Barker, 1999). Go to a movie, take a walk, meet a friend for coffee, or simply sit outside and enjoy the scenery—just get out and have some fun!

6) Set realistic limits. **Do not expect too much of yourself**. You need to avoid setting high goals at this time. You may need to cut back on some of your roles and responsibilities until your depression lifts.

7) **Avoid any extra stress**. Experts agree that, in order to recover, depressed people need a supportive environment that is free from distress and trauma. Also, you need to know your limitations, set boundaries with people, and become more comfortable with saying "no."

8) **Work on your spiritual life**: Interestingly, many professionals are encouraging people to develop their spiritual life to find overall health and balance (Flanagan, 2003; Koenig, et al, 1997). We believe that true emotional stability isn't possible without a solid, spiritual foundation. Your personal relationship with God is fundamental to living a healthy, balanced life. Building up your faith through Bible study, church attendance, prayer, and other spiritual activities will only enhance your sense of well-being.

*There are a number of sources in your community that can help you in this journey toward recovery from depression. Listed below are some of them:

- **Community Health Centers**: These facilities usually provide professional services at a low cost to the patient.
- **Family Service Agencies**: These organizations offer practical referrals that will be appropriate for your particular situation.
- **General Hospitals**: These medical facilities specialize in specific, short-term intensive care.
- **Mental Hospitals**: These medical facilities provide patient care to those with serious mental conditions.
- **Mental Health Clinics**: These clinics offer a wide variety of mental health services at an affordable cost to the patient.
- **Self-Help Groups**: Many self-help groups give assistance and support to individuals struggling with depression. Do not underestimate the value of support groups; they are useful forms of counseling.
- **Schools and Workplaces**: Many of these settings provide counseling or assistance programs for their students and employees. Most of them will offer referrals to qualified professionals in your area.
- **Suicide Prevention Hotlines**: These hotlines give immediate assistance during a crisis. You will find these numbers in your telephone book or from most medical and mental health facilities in your area. ***You can also dial 911 anywhere in the United States in an emergency to get help.***
- **Churches and Spiritual Leaders**: Most churches and religious organizations have information available and can offer support. Many people start here when seeking a solution to their emotional and psychological concerns. Finding a person of faith to walk with you through these challenging times will benefit you tremendously. Also, many

churches have staff members who have been trained to provide support and services to meet challenging circumstances. There may be support groups in place, or the church personnel may be able to direct you to a good source of help in your community.

There are a number of people who are qualified to treat you or someone you know with depressive disorders. Professional counselors have studied human behavior and have conducted supervised residencies and internships in preparation for public service. They are officially licensed by the state in which they practice. Below is a list of the disciplines in which many of these professionals have studied. Each discipline has an area of expertise and will take a specific approach to assisting you in the recovery process.

Marriage and Family Therapists: These counselors focus on relational issues. Family therapists have educational and clinical backgrounds in the areas of individual, marital, and child psychological needs.

Psychologists: Professionals educated and trained to provide diagnostics and treatment to those in mental and psychological distress. They provide valuable testing to determine psychological problems and will focus on specific treatment plans based on those findings.

Psychiatrists: Psychologists and psychiatrists differ in training and approach. A psychiatrist is a medical doctor who treats mental disorders from a medical model. Psychiatrists typically diagnose mental illnesses, counsel patients, and prescribe medication.

Psychiatric Nurses: These registered nurses can provide counseling, education, and medication monitoring. Psychiatric nurses are found in hospitals and community clinics specializing in the treatment of mental disorders.

Social Workers: These professionals provide counseling, referrals, and other services. They are often associated with an agency, such as a hospital, clinic, or non-profit organization.

Your **primary care physician** can be a valuable resource in helping to determine which referral is most appropriate for your mental health care.

Depression makes you feel exhausted and helpless; you will need the help of people who care about you.

Don't forget, family and friends can also play a major role in your recovery. Depression makes you feel exhausted and helpless; you will need the help of people who care about you. Remember, if the people supporting you have never been depressed, they might not understand your situation. You may want to give them a copy of this book in order to assist them in helping you through the healing process.

What If a Friend or Family Member Is Depressed?

One of the most loving things you can do for depressed individuals is make sure that they receive the appropriate treatment. You can encourage them to make an appointment to seek advice and even accompany them to the doctor's office. Loved ones and friends can also monitor an individual's progress to ensure that he or she is following the prescribed treatment plan.

Emotional support from family and friends is vital during treatment and recovery. Engaging the depressed person in conversation and activity can be helpful. Understanding, patience, affection, and encouragement are also important components of the recovery process.

Remember that all talk about suicide is serious. If someone you know talks about harming themselves, report it immediately to a mental health care provider or to the police. Suicide hotlines are available in most communities, so be aware of these resources and access numbers. Usually with treatment, depression improves within several weeks. Some helpful suggestions for alleviating depression are listed below. You can customize this list to meet your needs or those of a friend or loved one.

Helpful Hints for Healing from Depression

- Obtain a complete physical examination.
- Get a psychological evaluation.
- Set realistic and achievable goals.
- Don't take on too much responsibility.
- Set your priorities. Which responsibilities can you do without right now?

- Do not expect too much of yourself during recovery.
- Don't isolate yourself; get together with other people who care about you.
- Actively participate in pleasurable activities.
- Exercise four times each week.
- Practice proper nutrition.
- Don't make any major life decisions.
- Don't try to snap out of your depression; people seldom do.
- Don't accept negative thinking.
- Share your thoughts and feelings with others.

Medication

Successful treatment for depression may include medication, counseling, or a combination of the two. When properly addressed, depression can often be treated successfully without hospitalization.

Medications used to treat depression are called antidepressants. While there is no such thing as a happy pill, these medications are

> ***Successful treatment for depression may include medication, counseling, or a combination of the two.***

intended to ease the symptoms of depression and to assist a person in returning to healthy, day-to-day functioning. ***Antidepressant medications are not physically habit forming.*** However, it is important that the prescription is followed carefully.

Many people try to play doctor with their antidepressant medication. This can be dangerous! Depressive symptoms can intensify or you may experience no change at all if the medication is not properly administered. The patient also should be aware that alcohol should not be used in conjunction with these medications. All other drugs being taken, prescription or otherwise, need to be disclosed to your physician.

The side effects of antidepressants are usually minimal and should be discussed directly with your physician. These medications may cause mild and temporary side effects in some people, which are often more annoying than serious. It's recommended that patients weigh the relief that the medication gives them against the side effects—a process in which the prescribing physician will be able to assist. Typical side effects from some older medications include dry mouth, constipation, bladder problems, and sexual difficulties, as well as blurred vision, dizziness, and drowsiness. The newer generation of medications have different side effects, including headaches, nausea, insomnia, nervousness, and agitation.

Some people have concerns about taking psychiatric medications. They believe that weakness is associated with taking any drug. Others fear that their doctor will over-medicate them, and this would only complicate their problems. Technology has given us the miracle of medications to use in the healing process of many diseases. It's our belief that, when used properly, antidepressant medications can bring back emotional stability to a life that feels out of control. Any concerns about medication should be discussed directly with your physician. Don't forget, patience may be needed in order to find the correct medication and dosage that will give you the greatest benefit possible.

What Does the Bible Say About Depression?

Depression has impacted mankind from the beginning of time, and the Bible is full of examples and direct references to this disorder. These examples may encourage you as you look for hope and healing in dealing with depression.

Many of us have journeyed through the familiar "valley of the shadow of death" that David referred to in Psalm 23. Evangelist D.L. Moody said that God was evidently present in the valley that David described; otherwise, there would have been no shadows! Everyone experiences their own "valleys" at some point in their lives, but some people of faith believe that depression is something that only non-believers face. In fact, a few think that if only they were a little closer to God or a bit "more spiritual,"

Many of our Biblical heroes struggled with depression throughout their lives here on earth.

they would never suffer from troubling times. Well-intentioned Christians sometimes advise a depressed friend to simply pray, fast, or walk closer to God, and then the depression will lift. Not only does this ignore many of the real reasons we've discussed for the origination of this disorder, it is also hurtful to the person who is suffering from depression.

Does depression indicate weak faith? Is it a mark of some spiritual flaw? Nothing in Scripture supports this view. You may be surprised to find that many of our Biblical heroes struggled with depression throughout their lives here on earth.

Problems of living are common to all of us; they're not always about our personal weaknesses or errors. Many of life's afflictions, trials, disappointments, and depression are simply due to living in an imperfect world. This membership in the human dilemma includes living in an evil world. Christians are not exempt from suffering. In fact, Scripture guarantees suffering to Christians!

In their book, *Conquering Depression*, Sutton and Hennigan (2000) remind us that the Bible can help provide strength and support through seasons of depression. One way is to study the lives of people, just like us, who lived, struggled, and overcame their dilemmas with God's help. Let's look at a few examples:

Jonah was angry and depressed after God refused to destroy Nineveh.

The great prophet **Jeremiah** regretted the day that he was born.

Job was ridiculed by his wife and friends after he lost all his possessions, property, health, and family. In misery, he fell into depression.

Sarah was distraught because she couldn't have a baby. She then became depressed when her servant had a child by her husband (even though this was at her own request).

Naomi was despondent after the deaths of her husband and two sons while living in a foreign country.

Nehemiah was so depressed about the captivity of the people of Israel that the king saw it on his face.

The **Apostle Paul** was so downtrodden that he "despaired even of life."

A famous Biblical story regarding depression is found in the Old Testament. Let's look at the story in I Kings 19.

Long ago, a drought and famine had ravaged Israel over a three year period. Without rain, no crops would grow in the arid land, and the ensuing food shortages meant that many would die. The people were being judged by God for their disobedience, for worshipping idols, and for making human sacrifices to other gods. The prophet of God's people, **Elijah**, had a job to do. He challenged the king of Israel, Ahab, to a showdown because of all of the evil he and his queen, Jezebel, had allowed to happen in their country. Elijah claimed to be the only prophet of God left in Israel, and he was ready to oppose the 500 false prophets of the god, Baal, to demonstrate that his God was the only true God. Elijah challenged the king to call these prophets together and build an altar, and he would do the same. They would then call down fire from heaven, and whoever succeeded was the representative of the true God.

King Ahab took the challenge. The prophets of Baal called upon their god for half a day, even cutting themselves with knives to get his attention. Elijah stood by and watched the chaotic scene, asking them where their god was now that they truly needed him.

Then Elijah stepped to center stage. He dug a ditch around his altar and repeatedly dowsed it with water. He cried out to heaven, and fire came down and consumed the altar, the sacrifice, and all of the water. The people of Israel were amazed and immediately repented of their wickedness. Elijah ordered them to gather the 500 false priests of Baal and kill each and every one of them.

But the day wasn't finished yet. Elijah told King Ahab to find his chariot and get out of town because the draught was over—God was sending rain. And rain it did! God provided salvation in response to the repentance of His people.

A serious problem arose after this amazing event— instead of rejoicing in victory, Elijah quickly fell into despair. Queen Jezebel heard about her priests' humiliation and execution at the hand of God. As a foreigner, Jezebel had played a key role in reintroducing pagan worship in Israel, so she took the offence personally and vowed to kill Elijah. The word spread quickly.

Elijah, on top of the world one minute, was running for his life the next. He ran and hid in the desert where he was so depressed that he prayed for the Lord to take his life. Talk about coming

> ***The Lord provided nutrition, spiritual enrichment, exercise, and fellowship.***

down off the mountain top. The day's miraculous victory was completely forgotten because of his current circumstances.

What did God do for this depressed—even suicidal—man?

The Lord provided nutrition, spiritual enrichment, exercise, and fellowship. God, who had sent the fire and the rain, gave Elijah what he needed to survive this difficult time. He even sent an angel who provided food, rest, forty days of exercise, and later, the fellowship and encouragement from friends that he needed. Sounds like a pretty good treatment plan.

Elijah was depressed at a time when he logically should have been rejoicing. Instead, he wanted to die. But, if you notice, the Lord didn't rebuke him. God didn't ask Elijah to snap out of his depression. Instead, He met his needs and delivered him from his sorrows over time.

If a hero like Elijah can deal with depression, so can we!

Concluding Thoughts About Depression

Feelings of emptiness, loneliness, and meaninglessness are universal, and depression is as old as human history. It knows no boundaries and affects people of all ages, genders, ethnicities, and backgrounds. Depression is not always explainable, and it can strike even when things seem to be going well, but the great news is that we have discovered a tremendous amount of information about this disorder. Help and hope are available to anyone struggling with depression.

Help and hope are available to anyone struggling with depression.

The vignettes at the beginning of this book represent a small sampling of the reasons people become depressed. These individuals needed to take proactive steps in dealing with their depression. Here are a few of the results of their efforts:

Though recovery was abruptly halted by the loss of her husband, Tina determined to finish what she had started. A combination of therapy and medication helped her work through the major depression she was dealing with. Tina also found healing through her faith, joining a support group and a women's Bible study at her church.

For about two years, Keith's counseling dealt intensively with his past trauma and abuse. Though relationships were still difficult for him, Keith continued to work hard at developing intimacy with his wife, family, and friends.

Initially Mark sought help for his depression, but then he used his work schedule as an excuse to stop therapy. Unfortunately, today he is still struggling with many of the same issues, bewildered about why he feels so unhappy.

Lori has remained sober since she started counseling. Her hard won success came by understanding the role her family history played in her life and how chemical dependency impacted her personal relationships. Lori also decided to reconnect with God, and she is actively involved in her church. While still struggling with some anxiety issues, her depression has lifted—and she's found a new job.

Everyone who deals with depression has his or her own story, and the journey to recovery will be just as unique. By following the guidelines in this book, you can start your healing process, too. Remember, you're not alone in your struggles! Many people, past and present, have dealt with similar issues and have successfully battled this disorder.

You're not alone in your struggles! Many people, past and present, have dealt with similar issues and have successfully battled this disorder.

In addition, God has provided family, friends, and medical experts who are willing to help you. These men and women will be your greatest allies as you fight this enemy that can rob you of the joy that life should bring each and every day. You have taken the first important step toward healing—getting the information you need to start the process. There is hope for a brighter future. Our prayer is that you will continue on this path toward dealing with depression and enjoy the full, satisfying life God has planned for you.

God's Positive Answer to Our Negativity

For all the negative things we have to say to ourselves, God has a positive answer for it.

You say: "It's impossible."
God says: All things are possible. (Luke 18:27)

You say: "I'm too tired."
God says: I will give you rest. (Matthew 11:28-30)

You say: "Nobody really loves me."
God says: I love you. (John 3:16 & John 13:34)

You say: "I can't go on."
God says: My grace is sufficient. (II Corinthians 12:9 & Psalm 91:15)

You say: "I can't figure things out."
God says: I will direct your steps. (Proverbs 3:5-6)

You say: "I can't do it."
God says: You can do all things. (Philippians 4:13)

You say: "I'm not able."
God says: I am able. (II Corinthians 9:8)

You say: "It's not worth it."
God says: It will be worth it. (Romans 8:28)

You say: "I can't forgive myself."
God says: *I forgive you*! (I John 1:9 & Romans 8:1)

You say: "I can't manage."
God says: I will supply all your needs. (Philippians 4:19)

You say: "I'm afraid."
God says: I have not given you a spirit of fear. (II Timothy 1:7)

You say: "I'm always worried and frustrated."
God says: Cast all your cares on *me*. (I Peter 5:7)

You say: "I don't have enough faith."
God says: I've given everyone a measure of faith. (Romans 12:3)

You say: "I'm not smart enough."
God says: I give you wisdom. (I Corinthians 1:30)

You say: "I feel all alone."
God says: I will never leave you or forsake you. (Hebrews 13:5)

Turning My Trials into Triumph

Pain and suffering. Trial and tribulation. Difficult times are simply part of the journey through life. Along with the joys comes sadness; along with the blessings there are burdens.

Many people have a difficult time understanding how a loving God can allow pain and suffering to occur in our world. They sincerely ask, "Why me?" Men and women of all ages want to come to terms with their anger, fear, hurt, and confusion—and their desire to have a relationship with God.

Suffering is one of the "mysteries" that will only be fully understood when we get to Heaven, but many of the answers to life's dilemmas can be found in the Bible. We have outlined principles we've found in Scripture to help you process some of the questions you may have been asking. We hope they will assist you in understanding the role problems and pain play in our lives. You may discover, as we have, that suffering is part of a much bigger plan for our personal development. God loves you and has a purpose for everything that you go through in life.

He Suffered

The writer of Hebrews makes it absolutely clear that Jesus suffered when He lived on Earth. He endured the same kinds of trials and tribulations that we do, yet was without sin (Hebrews 2:18; 4:15-16). The book of Hebrews also tells us that Jesus personally understands our weaknesses because He suffered, so He will never leave us nor forsake us in our own suffering (Hebrews 13:5).

We Suffer

In one of his letters, the Apostle Peter talks about pain and suffering in life (I Peter 4:12-17). He explained these important points:

- Christians should not be surprised when they suffer.
- Suffering starts with Christians and moves to the world. God allows it in order to perfect our relationship with Him and point us in His direction.
- Suffering should not be strange to us. We should expect it as part of a plan for perfection in our lives.
- We should thank God for the opportunity to serve Him by suffering. The Gospels make it clear that suffering and Christianity go together. Christ suffered, so we have His example to follow.

He Wants to Help Us

- God is unique and has His own way of doing business with us (Isaiah 46:9). God created us with a specific purpose in mind—His purpose. Suffering is our opportunity to learn to live within His plan, instead of our plan (Proverbs 16:9).
- God refines and perfects us by allowing suffering in our lives (Isaiah 48:10). He wants to get our attention so that He can clearly reveal His love for us. Pain and suffering are designed to help us focus and get our attention on important opportunities so that God can fully demonstrate His love to us.
- God is our personal fortress and source of help (Psalm 46:1). Although we will struggle in our daily lives, God is always present to help us through difficult times.
- God has special plans for each of us; our best days lie ahead of us (Jeremiah 29:11). A common theme throughout Scripture is that we were chosen by God Himself to bring glory to His name (Ephesians 1:4). But He didn't stop there. Not only did God choose us, but He also designed

our lives to accomplish a specific purpose (or set of purposes) and for a glorious future (Ephesians 4:4).

- God wants to bear our burdens so that we don't have to (I Peter 5:7). He is the source of our strength (Psalm 46:1). God requests that we give all of our concerns about our lives to Him because He wants to carry all of our daily burdens.

It's important to note that all pain and suffering have a spiritual foundation. They are present in the world as the direct result of evil. Evil perverted God's original plan of innocence when Adam and Eve chose to disobey Him in the Garden of Eden (Genesis 1- 3, Romans 5-6). This history lesson is essential because without recognizing the existence of evil, we can't understand its impact on our lives.

Can I Have a Personal Relationship with God?

This is *the* most important question that you will ever ask, because your eternal destiny rests in the answer. One hundred years from today it's the only question and answer that will matter to you! **No other decision will compare to the significance of knowing where you will spend eternity after your life is over on this earth.**

The Bible has the answer to this question: You can have a personal relationship with God because He wants to have one with you! In fact, God sent His Son, Jesus, to die on the cross for our mistakes because He loves us and wants to save us from the consequences of evil. Your belief in Him alone is all that He asks.

Look at these simple steps, and answer this question once and for all:

1. **Let God SEARCH your heart.**
   Psalm 139:23-24—"Search me, O God, and know my heart; test me and know my anxious thoughts. See if there is any offensive way in me, and lead me in the way everlasting."

2. **SURRENDER your life to God:**
   John 14:6—"Jesus answered, 'I am the way and the truth and the life. No one comes to the Father except through me.'"

3. **WALK in the SPIRIT:**
   Galatians 3:24-25—"So the law was put in charge to lead us to Christ that we might be justified by faith. Now that faith has come, we are no longer under the supervision of the law."

Saying a simple prayer, such as the one that follows, is all that you need to accept Jesus as your Lord and Savior:

> *Dear Jesus, I know that I am a sinner, and I need You in my life to be saved from eternal separation from You. Forgive me of my sinful ways, Lord; cleanse my heart and bring me into Your family. I want to spend eternity with You! Thank You, Jesus, for saving me. I will follow You the rest of my days.*

Did you make this eternal decision? Awesome! You are now one of God's children, and you will be with Him for all of eternity. Share this decision with someone you know. Begin reading the Bible so the Lord can guide you about how to live your life for Him. Get involved in a local church so you can find Christian friends.

Contact us with news of your decision. If you have any questions, we would like to support you by sending some materials to start your new relationship with God!

SONKIST MINISTRIES

www.sonkist.com

Sonkist Ministries has a threefold mission: to encourage and motivate men and women to develop a close, personal relationship with Jesus Christ; to assist individuals, couples, and families in attaining spiritual and emotional balance; and to provide products and services that support the great news that the Gospel of Jesus Christ brings to our families, friends, and communities.

References

Agency for Healthcare Research and Quality, www.ahrq.gov.

Barker, S.B. (1999). Therapeutic aspects of the human-companion animal interaction. *Psychiatric Times*, 16(2), www.psychiatrictimes.com.

Baumeister, R.F., and Leary, M.R. (1995). The need to belong: desire for interpersonal attachments as a fundamental human motivation. *Psychological Bulletin*, 117 (3): 497-529.

Blumenthal, J., et al. (1999). Effects of exercise training on older patients with major depression. *Archives of Internal Medicine*, 159: 2349-2356.

Chambers, O. (2008). *My Utmost for His Highest.* Grand Rapids, MI: Discovery House Publishers.

Clay, R. (2001). Green is good for you. *Monitor on Psychology*, 32(4), www.apa.org.

Delate, T., Gelenberg, A.J., Simmons, V.A., and Motheral, B.R. (2004). Trends in the use of antidepressants in a national sample of commercially insured pediatric patients, 1998 to 2002. *Psychiatric Services*, 55: 387-391.

DSM-IV-TR: Diagnostic and Statistical Manual of Mental Disorders. 4th ed. (2000). Washington, D.C.: American Psychiatric Publishing.

Family First Aid, www.familyfirstaid.org.

Flanagan, O. (2003). The colour of happiness. *New Scientist*, 178 (2396): 44.

KidsHealth, www.kidshealth.org.

Koenig, H.G., et al. (1997). Modeling the cross-sectional relationships between religion, physical health, social support, and depressive symptoms. *American Journal of Geriatric Psychiatry,* 5: 131-143.

Krugman, S.D., & Dubowitz, H. (2003). Failure to thrive. *American Family Physician,* 68 (5) (September): 879-884.

LaHaye, T. (1996). *How to Win Over Depression*. Grand Rapids, MI: Zondervan.

Mayo Clinic, www.MayoClinic.com

National Healthcare Quality Report (2003). www.ahrq.gov.

National Institute of Mental Health, www.nimh.nih.gov.

National Mental Health Association, www.nmha.org.

Spurgeon, C. H. (2004). *The Treasury of David: Spurgeon's Classic Work on the Psalms.* Grand Rapids, MI: Kregel Publications.

Substance Abuse and Mental Health Services Administration, www.samhsa.gov.

Sutton, M.A., & Hennigan, B. (2000). *Conquering Depression: A 30-Day Plan to Finding Happiness.* Nashville, TN: B&H Publishing Group.

Tan, S.Y. (1995). The ABCs of depression: a review of the basics. *Christian Counseling Today:* 10-13.

United States Department of Health and Human Services, www.nhs.gov.

Welch, E.T. (2004). *Depression: A Stubborn Darkness—Light For the Path.* Greensboro, NC: New Growth Press.

World Health Organization, www.who.int.

Wright, H.N. (1976). *An Answer to Depression.* Eugene, OR: Harvest House Publishers.